ALL-AGE
ADVENT · CHRISTMAS

Ideas, talks and games for services

NICK HARDING

kevin mayhew

First published in 2002 by
KEVIN MAYHEW LTD
Buxhall, Stowmarket, Suffolk IP14 3BW
Email: info@kevinmayhewltd.com

9 8 7 6 5 4 3 2 1 0

ISBN 1 84003 949 3
Catalogue No. 1500529

Cover design by Angela Selfe
Edited and typeset by Elisabeth Bates
Printed and bound in Great Britain.

Contents _____

About the author _____

Nick Harding grew up in Birmingham, where he learned about Christianity from an early age. After going through the education system he taught in Nottinghamshire and has worked with a number of Christian organisations in a variety of roles ever since. Nick writes articles for a range of magazines and has written many books for and about working with children. He works as Children's Mission Support Officer for Southwell Diocese, supporting rural and urban churches in their work. Nick is a fan of the music of Elton John and Elgar, enjoys working out at the gym and walking in Sherwood Forest, and shares his life with his wife Clare, and sons Jared and Callum.

Introduction

There is so much to do at this time of year, and so much preparation to go through. We create things in our churches to busy ourselves, with Christingle services, Carol services, and other such activities. Now should be an opportunity to take stock, have a moment to breathe, and prepare ourselves spiritually for the light of Christ entering our world.

The Anglican Lectionary takes a double line on Advent, with readings relating both to the original coming of Christ, which we celebrate at Christmas, and to the final coming of Christ, which those in the early Church looked for, and we should look for too.

There will be those in most congregations who are already wrapped up in Christmas tinsel, even though Advent has only just begun. If they have fallen for the way the world 'does' Christmas they will have been dancing around supermarkets to the bland music versions of Christmas songs since the summer! We have a big task in working with our churches and all the people in them, young and old. Our challenge is to help them take a fresh look at the Advent season and prepare for the coming of Christ into their lives on 25 December, and every day.

This book contains many suggestions to help all-age Advent services and activities. There are games to do with some or all of the congregation, prayers to learn, repeat or use from the front, opening prayers and sentences in accessible language, and activities for family groups and others to do during a service. There are also talk suggestions and out-lines. There is enough here to keep your church going for many Advent and Christmas seasons in the future.

Activities and games _____

This range of activities and games is designed to be used with the congregation, and many encourage the congregation to get into groups or pairs. Some require prepared items and equipment, which are always listed at the beginning of each suggestion.

Wrap it up

You will need: 2 large boxes, 2 rolls of sticky tape, 2 pairs of scissors and 2 large rolls of wrapping paper.

Ask for two pairs of people to come to the front as volunteers. Then split the congregation into two, and encourage them to shout and cheer for one of the pairs each.

The pairs have three minutes to wrap the large box with paper as neatly as possible. Then you or a senior member of the congregation can judge how well they have done.

Fast food

You will need: 2 loaves of bread, 2 spreading knives, 2 jars of jam, on a table.

Ask for two families to come to the front as volunteers, and split the congregation up to cheer for one family each.

Place the bread as far away from the front as possible. You may be able to persuade two sidespersons to stand at the back with it. The two families have three minutes to make as many jam sandwiches as possible, collecting one slice of bread at a time.

Quick cards

You will need: sheets of A3 paper or thin card, marker pens.

Ask the congregation to get into groups of about five or six, with families and all ages mixing. Encourage family groups to 'adopt' single and older people into their groupings. Make sure that each group has a sheet of paper or card and two marker pens. Then ask them to discuss what to include on a Christmas card, and then draw and write on the paper or card. Once the cards are completed they should be brought to the front and shown to the others in the congregation.

Talk about getting ready

You will need: the questions below on OHP.

Introduce a discussion activity by mentioning some of the preparation that goes into Christmas. Then invite the congregation to get into small groups and family groups to think through some of these questions. Ask these questions as points of discussion:

- How should we prepare for Christmas?
- Did God mean Christmas to be like this?
- What is Advent really all about?
- What can we do as a church to make Advent more meaningful?
- What can we do as individuals to be prepared for Christmas?

My preparation

You will need: a sheet of paper with 1-10 on it for everyone, pencils, OHP (optional).

Give each member of the congregation a piece of paper with the numbers 1-10 on it. Ask them to talk with one or two around them, with younger people being helped and encouraged by older ones. They should write down 10 things that it is important to do before Christmas comes. They can write secular things (buying presents, etc.) and spiritual things too.

Once everyone has had some time to do this, ask some of them to shout out the things they have put on their lists, and if possible write up some of the responses on OHP.

Full of joy

You will need: balloons, permanent marker (OHP) pens.

Give out balloons to the congregation, at least enough for one to every three or four people. Ask those who receive a balloon to blow it up and tie it. If time is limited have some balloons blown up ready.

Then give each group a permanent marker or OHP pen. Talk about all the things that are good about Christmas time – joy, friends, parties, food, Jesus, services, etc. – and then give them a few minutes to write as many of these things as they can think of on the balloons. Children should be encouraged to have a go at this activity.

Once everyone has had a chance to write, the balloons should be thrown into the air and bounced around amongst the people. The balloons should then be collected in for the next activity, later in the service.

Bursting with joy

You will need: balloons written on (from 'Full of joy' activity).

Remind the congregation of the good things about the Advent and Christmas period. Explain that while the parties and fun soon pass, Jesus remains with us, and if we are properly prepared by praying and being open to God we will always be full of joy.

Warn the congregation, and especially younger children, that there may be some big noisy bangs from bursting balloons. Then invite the children to come to the front and burst all the balloons.

Giving away

You will need: slips of paper for each of the congregation, pencils.

Remind the congregation that Advent is the time when we think about what to give other people. Ask the congregation, in pairs, including younger and older people, to discuss the best gift they could give to someone.

They should then each write on a slip of paper a gift they would like to give someone. Younger children will need help with this. Then the whole congregation should mix, sharing the 'peace' and exchanging the slips of paper with gifts written on them as they do so.

Ask them: Who offered the best gift to us all at Christmas time? How do you feel about your selection of gifts? How do you feel about what you gave?

Waiting for the baby

Ask a 'new' parent from the congregation or elsewhere to come to the service and be interviewed by the leader of the service about what it is like to be awaiting the arrival of a child, and the excitement of the birth.

Allow members of the congregation to ask questions, and challenge everyone to think about this: What would it have all been like for Mary and Joseph?

What is it all about?

You will need: a long length of wallpaper, items listed below, glue.

Lay out a length of thick wallpaper the length of the aisle that people use to get to their seats or pews. Try to make the roll secure by weights along the length, or by pinning it carefully to the carpet underneath. Stick on to it things to do with Christmas – wrapping paper, tinsel, Christmas tree branch, pictures of Santa, balloons, food wrappers, cards with no Christian meaning, etc. Also along the length, at random, place some question marks.

As people enter, ask them to walk up the aisle carefully, glancing down at some of the things that may remind them of Christmas time. Once everyone is sitting down ask whether they could shout out some of the things they saw on the roll, and perhaps suggest things that are missing. Conclude this by mentioning that it is common to have all those things but forget what part Jesus plays in Christmas.

Drawing on God

You will need: an easel or flipchart with a pad of paper, pens and pencils.

For the services during Advent, have two young people with sketching and writing skills out at the front. Ask them to sketch pictures to illustrate the main themes of each service, or write down the key words or main points of the service. Near the end of each service look at what they have done during that service and ask the congregation to use their work as a reminder and a focus for thought, prayer and reflection.

You are an angel

You will need: plenty of small angel-shaped cards, pencils.

Begin by reminding the congregation that an angel came to warn Mary that she was special and chosen by God. She was so special that she was going to give birth to the special baby, Jesus.

Ask the congregation to get into small family groups or pairs. In their groups they should think about one other person in the congregation who they think is special and chosen to do things by God, and write their name on the front of one of the cut-out 'angels'. After enough time has been given for this, one person from each family or pair should take the angel to the person they have chosen, and hand it over.

Packing the parcel

You will need: a CD as a present, plenty of sheets of wrapping paper, sticky tape, scissors.

Ask for five children to come out as volunteers, each of whom should also bring one adult with them to help them. Line up the five pairs facing the congregation, with the adults standing behind the children.

This is a reversed version of 'pass the parcel'. Give the pair at one end of the line a pile of wrapping paper, a CD, and a roll of sticky tape. The first pair must 'pack' the CD as best they can until the music starts, and then pass it all on until the music stops . . . and so on. Each time it reaches the end of the line it should be passed back the way it has come. The person packing when the wrapping paper is all used up has the choice of who in the church they want the CD to go to, and give reasons for their choice. They mustn't keep it for themselves!

Advent feast

You will need: the foods listed below or similar, boxes or bags.

Introduce this activity by explaining that Advent and Christmas are often times when we all enjoy eating lots of food. Some of us may eat too much, others will be sensible. Sometimes the food can take over from the real meaning of the season.

Provide 10 different items of food, each given a number and hidden in boxes or bags. Then ask for five volunteers to come to the front. The volunteers should choose two numbers and eat both of the food items together! You could come up with some interesting combinations. Food items could include: bread, curry, pizza, carrots, jelly, cornflakes, Marmite, jam, cold chips, cheese, and so on.

Going my way

Ask the members of the congregation to get into 'family' groups and other groups of four or five in each, with a range of ages. Ask them to discuss any journeys they will be going on during the weeks before Christmas. Many will be planning to visit relatives or go on shopping trips. Ask for a few people to shout out one of the journeys they will be taking, and ask each a few questions about their journey. Finish by reminding them that the Advent season is the time when, 2000 years ago, Mary and Joseph had a long journey to Bethlehem.

Silent night

You will need: OHP picture or large picture of a desert scene as the sun is setting.

Remind the group that at night in the desert areas between Nazareth and Bethlehem it would have been cold and very quiet.

Then ask everyone to be very quiet and either look at the picture or close their eyes and imagine the scene, with Mary and Joseph resting on their journey. During the time of quiet say the following phrases gently, in turn, allowing a few seconds to pass between each one:

The stars shine in the dark sky.

Mary looks up.

Joseph thinks of the God who made it all.

They have nothing to disturb their rest and peace.

Once the congregation begins to get restless ask them to open their eyes again. Explain that the activity was to help them spend time in silence focusing on God, in what is a very busy time for everyone.

Advent questions

You will need: prepared questionnaires devised by a children's group or youth group about Advent and preparation for Christmas. There should be enough copies for groups of three or four.

Ask the congregation to get into small groups to discuss and fill in the questionnaire about Advent and preparing for Christmas. If possible publish the answers in the church newsletter.

What's in the news?

You will need: newspaper and chocolate bars.

Ask for two volunteers and stand them facing the congregation. Stand behind them and read them a headline, asking each of them in turn to say what the news item may be. Repeat this with different headlines a few times. At the end give them both a chocolate bar as a 'prize'. Finish by reminding the congregation that Advent is about preparing to hear the best news of all – the birth of Jesus.

Advent crown

You will need: an advent crown with five candles.

During Advent have an Advent crown at the front of the church for people to look at and use as a focus for prayer. You may want to begin the services during Advent by lighting the appropriate candles. If so, make sure that a range of people of all ages is invited to light the candle, helping those who may not be able to do it on their own.

Advent moments

You will need: a watch with a second hand, a gong or whistle and small prizes.

Invite three people to come to the front. They should then talk for 30 seconds each on one of the following subjects. If they stop talking before their time is up they have not won, but if they complete the 30 seconds you should bang the gong or blow the whistle and give them a prize.

Presents	Christmas food
Shopping	Nativity

Wonderful words

Plan and put on a service where members of the congregation are asked to bring along favourite passages of writing on the theme of Christmas and Advent. They may choose passages from the Bible, books or poems. Ask the children's groups in particular to contribute. Once each person has contributed, or an adult has read a section for the children, ask them to explain briefly why the writings mean something special to them.

Which wrapping?

You will need: a range of costumes similar to those listed below.

Invite three volunteers to come to the front. Place a range of different clothes and uniform items around. Explain to all the congregation that what we wear (literally, how we are wrapped up) tells others about us (e.g. the latest fashion – cool!). Then describe a person, and the volunteers must walk to the clothing that they think matches. An example could be a doctor's white coat – 'someone who cares . . . saves lives . . . holds surgeries . . .', etc. Other items of clothing could be an apron, a police hat, a nurse's watch, a clerical robe, a pin-striped suit, a car mechanic's overalls, and so on.

After the activity, explain that Jesus was wrapped up in ordinary cloth. His wrapping said that even though he was the Son of God, he was born as a baby just like all of us.

Advent things

You will need: two sheets of paper and pencils.

Invite two children to come out with an adult each to help them, and give each adult a piece of paper and a pencil. Then allow them one minute to write down as many things to do with each of the following subjects as possible, stopping after each one to see how they are doing and decide on the best or most original.

Winter	Parties
Presents	Shopping
Performance	Christmas carols

New start

Remind the congregation that although we often think of New Year as being the time for new beginnings, the church calendar sees Advent as the time to start again, preparing for the coming of Jesus.

Ask everyone to think of one thing they would like to try to do or be able to do better. Then count to three, asking everyone to say the thing they want to change, then start again with all speaking together. This may take a little practice, but do encourage everyone to join in.

'Myth or message' quiz

Split the congregation into two teams where they sit. Read each team one of the following statements in turn, and keep a score of right answers. Their task is to decide which of these statements are from the real story of Jesus in the Bible and which are myths that have built up around Christmas.

1. Jesus was born in a stable which was like a shed.
2. There were three wise men.

3. Mary rode to Bethlehem on a donkey.
4. Jesus was Mary's first child.
5. There were cattle in the stable.
6. The wise men visited them in a house.
7. The shepherds visited on the night Jesus was born.
8. The wise men visited on the night Jesus was born.
9. Mary thought deeply about the shepherds' visit.
10. The wise men were kings of lands in the East.

Numbers 1, 2, 3, 5, 8, and 10 are myths, some of which actually may be true, but there is no way of knowing! The others are biblically true.

Talks

These talks follow a range of styles from letters and monologues to be read out with little explanation, to clear talks based more on a sermon style. Like most resources, they will not all be ideal for your situation, and therefore may require some adaptation.

Jesus' wrapping

Who is looking forward to Christmas Day? It seems as if Christmas has been with us for a long time. Each year the signs of the season can be seen earlier, and tinsel appears in supermarkets next to the latest Christmas editions of magazines . . . in October! For many people, including your parents, it all gets too much, and by the time we get to celebrating everybody is tired and bad-tempered.

Then it comes to presents, and we look at the pile of them. There are presents that look really good, wrapped in expensive, shiny paper. And there are those that look tatty, wrapped in cheap paper.

With all the trimmings and wrappings it's too easy to forget Jesus. We throw away the truth of Christmas like the torn wrapping paper. (Tear some paper as you speak.)

We don't really know what the stable was like where Mary and Joseph were sent by the innkeeper. It would have been better to be inside a nice cosy house, but there was no room available, so a stable it had to be. Imagine what it must have been like for them, after walking such a long way, to have to settle and stay in a place where animals usually lived. The stable might have been a cave carved into the hillsides around Bethlehem. Or it might have been a rough wooden shed. It would have been cold, damp and draughty. It would have been smelly, cluttered and dirty. Yet it was somewhere for Mary and Joseph to sleep, and they were so tired that they were grateful for anything.

Finally, without the help of hospitals, doctors or midwives, the baby Jesus was born. Mary and Joseph must have been exhausted and delighted to see the tiny baby. He was and is God's Son, born to be King. But he wasn't wrapped up in expensive robes or furs as princesses and kings should be. He wasn't treasured by rich people. Instead, like any unimportant baby, he was wrapped up in cheap, common, ordinary cloths. Then he was placed in a feeding trough that was normally used by donkeys.

It is amazing that Jesus was wrapped up in such ordinary things, yet it tells us something about him. It tells us that he was born as an ordinary person, and he came to show us that he cares for ordinary people. His wrapping tells us that he knows what our lives are like, and that he cares about us.

Sandwich race

This talk is in three sections, and is based around the activity 'Fast food' on page 7.
You will need: a loaf of bread and jar of jam.

Who has heard their mums or dads complain about how much there is to do before Christmas? Who has heard them moan about how much it is all going to cost? Who has heard them say 'I'll never get everything done in time'? Who has heard their husbands or wives complain that it is all going to go wrong?

There is so much to do at this time of year, and so much preparation to go through. We have the busyness of Christmas services and performances at church, parties to go to, and lots of presents to buy. There is wrapping to be done, money to be spent, and food to be eaten. We are now in a special time of year. There are calendars named after this time. It is the Advent season, as we prepare for Christmas.

Game

Give the loaf of bread to a member of the congregation or a steward at the back of the church, and place the jar of jam on a table at the front. Invite two pairs of people to come out and help, the task of each pair being to make a better jam sandwich than the other. Give them one minute to run to the back, collect one slice of bread at a time, run to the front and spread some jam on the bread using their fingers! After one minute stop the race, have a look at how they are doing so far, and give Talk 1.

Talk 1

The season of Advent is a bit like making a jam sandwich! We have lots to do, and it's all a bit of a race, like our two sandwich-makers. We have our normal life to go through, the ordinary things like school work, arguments at home, and fights with brothers or sisters. Our normal life that goes from day to day is like the bread. But there's something really good coming up, something really exciting, called Christmas. That's like the jam in the sandwich.

Game

Continue the game for another minute, and then stop again. Look at how the sandwiches are going (pretty messy probably) and show the others what they look like. Then move on to Talk 2.

Talk 2

With all the rushing around and getting things ready, like making sandwiches, we can forget what it is really all about. Rather than rushing during Advent we should be stopping and taking time to prepare ourselves for Christmas. It was Christmas time 2000 years ago when Jesus was born. He was the Son of God, and changed the world. We shouldn't be rushing around during Advent, we should be thinking about Jesus, and how we will greet him at Christmas time.

Game

Continue for one more minute, and then stop. Look at the two sets of sandwiches, and decide which are the best. Then either throw them away there and then, or (if you are very brave) eat them! Continue into Talk 3.

Talk 3

After all that rushing around and fuss making the sandwiches they've gone! The two sandwich-makers have done so much preparation, but it's all been a bit of a waste of time!

Advent is the time God has given us to prepare to celebrate the birth of Jesus. If we forget Jesus during Advent we will do all our other preparation and work, buying presents and rushing around, but as soon as Christmas passes it will all seem like a waste of time. If we spend time in quiet and meet Jesus we will have something worthwhile left after Christmas. Advent is the time to get ready – not for sandwiches, food, parties and presents – but for Jesus. Let's start now!

Prepare the way

Photocopy Isaiah 52:7-10 to make enough copies for the congregation to work in family or other groups of around five in each, and cut it up line by line. Give the groups six minutes to work out how the verses go together, and to stick them in the correct order onto a piece of paper. You could make it more difficult by not telling them the Bible reference, and cutting off the verse numbers.

Once they have had enough time have someone else dash through the church doors and run from the back of the church up the aisle shouting, 'Get ready, be prepared. Good news is coming!' They should continue shouting the same phrases as they run around the church and then back out through the doors.

Once the person has gone, look in the direction of the doors with a bemused look on your face. Then go back to the reading from Isaiah, with everyone reading it together from their sheets and an OHP copy of it if available.

Explain that this is a prophecy in poetic language, and simply ask the groups to decide, 'Is it true?' Once they have had two minutes to decide, explain what it means in simple terms:

'the messenger' – John the Baptist

'good news' – Jesus, reflecting the language of the angels to the shepherds

'Jerusalem' – the holy city, representing the people of Israel

'all the world will see it' – the world was and is being changed by Jesus.

The challenge for all of us is to believe the message that the good news for all the world is coming, and take time to prepare ourselves for it.

Christingle

Christingle services occur in many churches and are part of the annual fundraising programme for the Children's Society. This talk outline is taken from my book *All-age Everything* (Kevin Mayhew, 2001).

This story and talk are combined, in three parts. Each should be based and told from a different area of the church. You will need the phrase CHRIST IN written up on a large sheet of paper and displayed, and the G, L and E on pieces of paper to put with it.

1. Christ in G: stand near the crib or tree if you have one in place. Ask a child to hold up the letter G. Explain that G is for gifts. Jesus was a gift that we remember at Christmas, as God sent Jesus as the best present we could ever have. But we all have gifts to use too that come from Jesus. We can share, love, care, etc. Christ is a gift from God, and gives us gifts.

2. Christ in L: stand near a candle. Ask a child to hold up the letter L. Explain that L is for light. Jesus brought light to the world. When he had grown up he went from town to town and village to village speaking to people, healing and helping them. He also explained who he was, on one occasion saying, 'I am the light of the world'. He brings light to the darkness and sad times in our lives. Jesus is the light, and brings light to our dark times.

3. Christ in E: stand amongst the congregation. Ask a child to hold up the letter E. Explain that E is for everyone. Because Jesus was the best gift, and because he brings light to all the world, we can all have Jesus with us. Another name for Jesus is Immanuel, which means 'God is with us'. Jesus wants to be with everyone, including all of us here. Jesus wants to be with everyone, but do we want Jesus?

Believing and Accepting

These talks could be combined and expanded into an adult sermon, delivered in two parts over two weeks, or used as a brief thought-starter for a service where a large number of visitors are present.

Believing

Readings: Isaiah 40:1-11, Luke 1:1-25

If time allows, practise the Luke reading with volunteers playing the roles of Zechariah, Elizabeth and Mary. They should act it out as it is read.

Elizabeth and Zechariah were not expecting to be parents, they thought they were too old. They believed in God, and Zechariah was an important person who worked in the Temple. On one particular day Zechariah had a special job to do in the Temple, and on going there was surprised to see an angel. It was unbelievable! As he slowly got over the shock, he was even more astonished to hear what the angel had to say. When he heard what the angel said – that he and Elizabeth would have a child – he couldn't believe it. Zechariah thought it was unbelievable! Then another unbelievable thing happened – he was struck dumb to give him time to think about the unbelievable things that were happening. Zechariah had certainly had an unbelievable morning!

The reading from Isaiah, written some 700 years before Jesus was born, is also pretty unbelievable! The voice cries out to us all to prepare a way for Jesus. The message is the same now as it was then. It was and is a message for all people. Do we believe that Jesus can come to us afresh this Advent? Are we ready to really believe that Jesus is ready to be welcomed again? Do we really believe that Jesus was willing to be born as a baby and die for us? Is that just too unbelievable?

Accepting

Readings: Isaiah 40:1-11, Luke 1:1-25

If time allows practise the Luke reading with volunteers playing the roles of Zechariah, Elizabeth and Mary. They should act it out as it is read, even if you did the same the week before.

Zechariah was struck dumb after hearing the amazing news that the angel had given. He had no choice but to accept that he was not going to be able to speak, and that the words of the angel were true. While he had silent time to think he accepted that God was in control, God was powerful, and God knew best. Elizabeth found the news that the angel gave difficult to accept at the beginning, but soon came to realise that God knew what was going to happen. She didn't ask, 'Why didn't I have a child younger?', or 'Why has God made this happen now?' She accepted that God was sending her a child, and God had his own reasons for it.

Isaiah 40:10-11 reminds us that God cares about us all as individuals. None of us is too bad or too good, too holy or too nasty to be able to accept that God really loves us. In a world where people get hurt and find it hard to trust, Jesus comes to gather us together as sheep and to protect us. We can disagree with it, argue against it, or accept it. Accepting it is the best way to go, not just for this Advent, not just for Christmas, but for all of our lives.

Zechariah and Elizabeth learned to believe and accept the power and love of God. This Advent we can come to believe and accept that Jesus came to meet us. The choice of whether to believe and accept is up to you.

Christmas N

This is an all-age service that could include a nativity as a part of it. If you choose to do the nativity section then all the usual costumes will need to be prepared in advance for angels, shepherds, Mary, Joseph, a 'baby', and the wise men. If possible, include older members of the congregation as well as children in the nativity scene. There should also be one or two adults who are willing to help position the nativity characters at the appropriate point during Talk 3.

Prepare a large 'N' out of thick card, paint in bright colours, and put up as high as possible at the front of the church.

Reading: Isaiah 11:1-9

Talk 1

'N' is for news. We have already heard some of the things that are in the news today, but what about the news a very long time ago, when Isaiah wrote the words we heard in the first reading? In the news 2,700 years ago was the prophet Isaiah, a messenger from God. He knew that many years after his time something amazing was going to happen. He gave news of a new leader who would be wise and full of knowledge. The new leader, as we heard in the reading, would bring peace to the world. This news was a surprise for the people, and as the news spread they wondered when it would all happen. This was news for everyone, news that would change the world, news that would mean things would never be the same again. 'N' is for News.

Talk 2

'N' is for news, the news that Isaiah brought to the people 2,700 years ago. And 700 years after that, just 2,000 years ago, 'N' is still for news. This time it is the news that Gabriel brought to Mary. It was news that was a shock to Mary, who was not expecting to have a baby. She was surprised to see an angel, and even more surprised that God had chosen her to be the mother of a special baby. It was news that was also a shock for Joseph, whom she planned to marry. It was news that was beyond anyone's understanding: news that the promised leader was coming. Mary celebrated the news by singing a song praising God with similar words to those we have just said in the Thanksgiving.

Talk 3

The 'N' still hangs up there. 'N' is for the news that Isaiah brought to all the people 2,700 years ago, that a new leader would be born. 'N' is for the news that Mary heard from Gabriel, that she would be the mother of a very special baby. 'N' is also for the nativity scene. First let's have Mary and Joseph, with the baby. They were at the centre of the nativity scene. Meanwhile on the hillside were shepherds, so the shepherds can come on now. They were ordinary people, not clever or rich. But still the news the angels had was for them, and they became part of the nativity. Then, some days later, wise men travelled to see the baby Jesus. Let's see our wise men. They had studied old writings and travelled a long way. They knew that the good news was for all people from all places.

The 'N' for nativity is a popular part of Christmas, and an important one as long as we remember that all the news was about the baby Jesus, the leader promised 700 years before.

Talk 4

'N' is for the news from Isaiah and the news that Gabriel gave Mary. 'N' is for the nativity scene we imagine, and we can see here. The final 'N' is for now. I wonder what is going through your mind now? Do you remember when you were in a nativity scene, or are you thinking about the presents you want or the preparations that still need doing? Now it is easy to miss Jesus in all the rush and fuss of Christmas.

All that news, and the first nativity, were all because of now. Jesus came to the world for everyone, and that includes us. Now we have the chance to put him at the centre of the nativity. Now we have a chance to put Jesus at the centre of our Christmas. Now we have the chance to put Jesus at the centre of our lives. The news was for us, the nativity was for us. Jesus is for us, now.

Who is Christmas for?

To make this talk visual you will need some people dressed as shepherds, and others as kings.

Who is Christmas for? We spend a lot of time and money on Christmas, and even now we are busy preparing for it. People say lots of different things about who Christmas is for, and here are some of them:

Christmas is for children. This is often said, and is partly true. It's true that children really enjoy the parties and presents, the performances and plays. But to say Christmas is only for children is a bit of an excuse from adults who don't really want to think about what God wants to say to them about Jesus being born for them.

Christmas is for families. Yes, it is true that Christmas is a time when we think of others in our families, and often families come together and meet up. We have big meals together, and see people we've not met all year or even longer. But sometimes being together isn't happy, and arguments can begin. Christmas is for families, but it is even more for individuals.

Christmas is for businesses. Yes, lots of businesses and people make money at this time of year. Christmas has become very commercialised and seems to be based around how much money we can spend and how much tinsel and food we buy. Christmas is important for businesses, but that is not what Christmas is really for. If we believe that Christmas is only about money and business we forget the truth.

So much for people's views on modern Christmas. Let us look at these, the shepherds and kings, and think more about the truth of Christmas.

Shepherds. Christmas is for people like these. People who are ordinary, go to work, are not necessarily famous or popular, and are not thought of as clever or special, are at the centre of the Christmas story. It was these ordinary people to whom the angels chose to give the good news. Jesus was born for people like these, and people like us. No one is too ordinary to be part of the true Christmas.

Kings. Christmas is also for people like these. There are important people in the world, and people who have a lot of power. There are many people who have a lot of money, and think they do not need anything else. But these kings went to the stable and knelt down to worship Jesus, showing that there are more important things than power or money. Christmas with Jesus at the centre is for people like these.

Look at the people around you. Christmas is for people like these! The people around you may be young or old, rich or poor, beautiful or . . .! They and you are what Christmas is all about. Jesus was born for all people, and remembering the time he was born at Christmas is for you and for all people in the world. It is no use coming out with excuses – Christmas is only about money, it is only for families, it is all about children – Christmas is for you. The question we all have to think about is whether we are ready to meet Jesus this Christmas.

It's time to get ready

This talk has a response for the congregation to learn before you begin and to say at appropriate points during the talk:

You: It's time to get ready.
All: It's time to get ready.

Prepare a rucksack or suitcase beforehand with things you would take on a journey or holiday. Basic items like clothes, toothpaste, money and so on would be fine.

I wonder how many of you will be going on journeys this Advent? I guess many of you will be piling into the car or jumping on a train to go off and do a little more shopping. As you prepare for your extra shopping trip you'll say, 'It's time to get ready . . .' You may be dashing off over the next few weeks to visit relatives or friends whom you have not seen for a while. There are presents to wrap and cards to write for them. It's time to get ready . . . You may be aiming to go away this Christmas, so you have to get ready for that. It's time to get ready . . .

I have a bag/case here which I have packed. I've decided to get ready, 'cos it's time to get ready . . . Here are some of the things I have prepared for the journey [take out the items one by one]. But during the first Advent there were journeys taking place too, and plenty of people who said it was time to get ready . . .

There were very clever, powerful men who had been studying stars, maps and charts for a long time. They thought that a very special star was going to appear, and they wanted to follow it to wherever it stopped. One said, 'It's time to get ready . . .' And so it was. They got ready and rode on a long journey westwards, following a star in the sky. During the day they would rest, and as it got darker they would say to each other, 'It's time to get ready . . .', and they would pack up their things and set off following the star in the dark, clear sky.

There was a young couple, Mary and Joseph. They knew that it was time for them to go on a journey to Bethlehem so that Joseph could be listed as one of the people in the country, as the law said. He said to Mary, 'It's time to get ready . . .', and that is what they did. They packed up all they could carry and set off on the long walk, which lasted days and days, to Bethlehem. When they got there they ended up having to take shelter in a stable, and then Mary said, 'It's time to get ready . . .' but this time she was talking about the birth of her baby.

Angels appeared on the hillside outside Bethlehem. They had come from God with a very special message. As a group of shepherds stared in amazement and surprise the angels said, 'It's time to get ready . . . for a new time when peace will be everywhere. It's time to get ready . . . for the baby who has just been born, and is a new King.' As the shepherds looked on the angels vanished. 'It's time to get ready . . .' said one shepherd, 'let's put the sheep safe and get going down to Bethlehem and find this baby.' Quickly they sorted the sheep out and went off to worship the baby Jesus.

'Let's get ready . . .' was a phrase used by the wise men as they prepared and set off to follow the star and finally to meet Jesus. 'Let's get ready . . .' was a phrase used by the shepherds as they ran down to find the stable and worship Jesus. 'Let's get ready . . .' was the phrase used by the angels to the shepherds, and to all people. They told us to get ready for the new King, Jesus. Are you ready?

Speechless!

This is the story of Zechariah, and the promise that God made to him. At the end there are some key points which could easily be expanded depending on the nature of the congregation. Tell this story, practising this response before you start:

Leader: It's enough to make you . . .

All: Speechless!

Zechariah was a priest, and he was old. His wife was Elizabeth, and she was old too! They had long since given up the idea of having children – the idea was so silly it's enough to make you . . . speechless! On one normal, everyday morning Zechariah was working away in the Temple as normal when he saw a vision, a person . . . an angel! It was enough to make you . . . speechless! He looked at the angel, and listened to what he said. The angel's message was clear – God had listened to their prayers and as a result Zechariah and Elizabeth were to have a child. The boy should be called John, and he would be a great servant of God and point many people the right way. After he heard this amazing news Zechariah couldn't really believe it – it was enough to make you . . . speechless. He asked the angel how it could possibly be – he was too old. The angel told Zechariah that because he didn't really believe it he would be speechless and unable to even mutter a word until it all happened . . . well, that's enough to make you . . . speechless!

Months passed, and old Zechariah couldn't say a thing – it's enough to make you . . . speechless! Finally his wife gave birth to a boy, and she had already decided that John would be a good name. But their friends and family were not impressed – it was enough to make you . . . speechless! No one in the family had ever been called John, and they didn't like the name. So everyone turned to the dumb priest Zechariah and asked him to write down the name for his son. 'John', he wrote. The crowd gasped in amazement as suddenly he could speak again – it was enough to make you . . . speechless! Then Zechariah used his new ability to speak again, and he spoke out a long prayer of praise to God.

And so John grew up under the care of his old parents Zechariah and Elizabeth, and did become a great servant of God. Such an incredible story – it's enough to make you . . . speechless!

We might be speechless when we open our presents this Christmas. We might be speechless at the decorations we see, the cost of the presents we want to buy, or the amount of food we are offered at special meals or parties. But Christmas should make us speechless as we think of God's Son Jesus being born as a baby. This Christmas we can have a powerful experience of Jesus that really will make us speechless!

Prayers _____

Advent is a key time to be quiet and listen to God, so prayer is of vital importance. This selection of prayers includes introductions, confessions, thanksgivings, intercessions and endings. They could be used on their own or supplemented by prayers from service books and *Common Worship*, or other prayers prepared by members of the congregation.

Opening sentences

'Comfort my people' says our God. 'Comfort my people now!'
(Isaiah 40:1)

This is good news about Jesus Christ, the Son of God.
(Mark 1:1)

Glory to God in heaven, and peace to all of his people on earth.
(Luke 2:14)

The one who is coming will baptise you with the Holy Spirit and with fire.
(Matthew 3:11)

My heart praises him, and my soul is glad because of God my Saviour.
(Luke 1:46-47)

Go up on a high hill and shout out the good news!
(Isaiah 40:9)

The Lamb of God, who takes away the sin of the world, is coming.
(John 1:29)

God has kept his promises, and has come to save his people.
(Luke 1:54)

Where is the king? We have come to worship him.
(Matthew 2:2)

Here is good news, which will bring great joy to all people.
(Luke 2:10)

The Lord will use his holy power and he will save his people.
(Isaiah 52:10)

The Lord is coming to rule all with power.
(Isaiah 40:10)

The Lord will gather his lambs together and care for them.
(Isaiah 40:11)

Do not be afraid. I have called you by name – you are mine!
(Isaiah 43:1)

There is nothing that our God cannot do.
(Luke 1:37)

A voice cried out: 'Get the wilderness road ready for the Lord.'
(Isaiah 40:3)

Prayers

We are waiting for the good news,
we are waiting.
We are waiting for the time of celebration,
we are waiting.
We are waiting for the son of man,
we are waiting.

Please be in us,
please be in us,
as we get ready,
as we get ready.

Please be with us,
please be with us,
as we worship,
as we worship.

Please speak to us,
please speak to us,
as we listen,
as we listen.

Prepare the way of the Lord.
Prepare ourselves in our minds, opening them to God.
Prepare ourselves in our hearts, opening them to God.
Prepare the way of the Lord.

As we sit in quietness
we will get ready, get ready for God.
As we put our thoughts aside
we will get ready, get ready for God.
As we calm our hearts
we will get ready, get ready for God.
As we think of worship
we will get ready, get ready for God.

The Lord is coming to save his people,
Jesus, please save me.
The Lord is coming to lead his people,
Jesus, please lead me.
The Lord is coming to love his people,
Jesus, please love me.

Prayer stones

Put a pile of small stones in the centre of the church. Ask the congregation to sit quietly and think about their personal spiritual preparation for Christ. Then invite them to come forward and take a stone to symbolise their personal commitment to remembering Jesus during Advent.

After a time of quiet remind the congregation that Advent leads to Christmas, and Christmas leads, eventually, to Jesus coming again. It is the start, not the end.

The Lord is coming,
he is coming.
The Lord will rule in power,
he is coming.
The Lord will gather us like sheep,
he is coming.
And he will be our shepherd,
he is coming.

Proclaim the message that the Lord is coming.
Let us be quiet and think about how we can proclaim Jesus (pause).
Proclaim the message that the Lord is coming.
Let us be quiet and think about how we can be open to Jesus (pause).
Proclaim the message that the Lord is coming.
Let us be quiet and wait for Jesus now (pause).
Proclaim the message that the Lord is coming.

Advent candle

Purchase an Advent candle, and use it in every service during Advent. As you darken the room and light the candle, encourage the congregation to remain quiet and look at the candle while you read out the passage from Luke 2:1-6. Some suitable quiet music may help to focus on Jesus.

Prepare in the wilderness a road for the Lord.
Prepare in our community an awareness of the Lord.

Prepare in our church a way for the Lord.
Prepare in our lives some space for the Lord.

Let us think of the things we are looking forward to.
Let us think of the fun, the parties, the feasts and the gatherings.
Let us think of the services, the celebrations and the carols.
Let us remember the baby, born for us.

We wait for the birth of Jesus.
We wait for the season of celebration.
We wait for the good news he brings.
We wait to be changed by him.

Let's be quiet for a while, and close our eyes to help us imagine. As we think about Christmas we picture the darkness of the stable, and Mary and Joseph watching the newborn baby in the manger. Now imagine the baby, wrapped up in ordinary cloths, not rich, fine garments.

What we are wrapped in says so much about us. Jesus was wrapped in an ordinary way so that ordinary people like us could know his love ... even in the wrapping of Christmas!

My soul is glad because God loves me.
My heart praises God.
From this moment on I will always be happy.
My heart praises God.
God shows he cares for those who follow him.
My heart praises God.
He brings good things to those in need.
My heart praises God.
He always keeps his promises.
My heart praises God.
God will never forget us.
My heart praises God.

Let's think of all the things we are looking forward to this Christmas.
Now let's think of that baby, Jesus, born at Christmas time so long ago.

Thank you, Jesus, that you came to our world. Help us all to prepare for you this Advent. Amen.

Intercessions

We pray for all people who do not know the news that Jesus lives for them.
Jesus, **Jesus, be with us and hear us now.**
We pray for all people who have had bad, sad and upsetting news.
Jesus, **Jesus, be with us and hear us now.**
We pray for places in the news where there is no peace today.
Jesus, **Jesus, be with us and hear us now.**
We pray for ourselves at this Christmas time.
Jesus, **Jesus, be with us and hear us now.**
We pray that the nativity will mean more than ever before.
Jesus, **Jesus, be with us and hear us now.**
We pray that you would be the centre of our lives now.
Jesus, **Jesus, be with us and hear us now.**

We think of those who do not enjoy preparing for Christmas. We pray for those who are lonely, sad or ill. In particular we pray for . . .
We think of those who are having a hard time this Christmas. We pray for those who have no money, no home, or no family. In particular we pray for . . .
We think of those who do not understand Christmas. We pray for those who blame God for hard times, or have no one to share Christmas with. In particular we pray for . . .
We think of ourselves as we get ready for Christmas. We pray that we will all find time to make room for Jesus.

We pray for our world, that people who suffer would be helped.
We pray to you this Advent.
We pray for our country, that it would look to you at this time.
We pray to you this Advent.
We pray for our church, that we would share the good news.
We pray to you this Advent.
We pray for ourselves, that we would welcome Jesus again.
We pray to you this Advent.

As we pray for ourselves and bring you our needs
help us, Jesus, at this special time.
As we pray for our church family and bring you our needs
help us, Jesus, at this special time.
As we pray for our community and bring you our needs
help us, Jesus, at this special time.
As we pray for our world and bring you our needs
help us, Jesus, at this special time.

Responses for intercessions

Lord, hear us as you come to us.

We bring these prayers to you, hear us this Christmas we pray.

We pray to you this Advent.

As we prepare for you, help us we pray.

Lord Jesus, born as a baby, please hear our prayer.

Please God, who gave your Son, hear us and help us.

Lord, in your mercy and love, hear our prayer.

As we are quiet please hear us, Lord.

Jesus, come to us and help us we pray.

At this special time please bring your light.

Endings

So may the joy of the news from the Father, the excitement of the nativity of the Son, and the strength of the Holy Spirit now, be with us this Christmas and evermore. Amen.

Jesus is coming,
let us prepare for him. Amen.

May the coming of Jesus encourage us.
May the coming of Jesus help us.
May the coming of Jesus change us. Amen.

May the blessing of the Father who sent his Son,
the Son who came as a baby,
and the Holy Spirit who remains in us,
be with us all evermore. Amen.

Let us go from here and prepare the world to meet Jesus.
Let us go from here and prepare ourselves to meet Jesus.

Jesus came to the world to save us and change us.
Let us allow him to save us and change us.

As we prepare for Christmas time
send us out to get ready for you.
As we prepare in church and at home
send us out to get ready for you.
As we prepare in our minds and hearts
send us out to get ready for you.

Be with us, Lord, as we go into this busy world.
Be with us, Lord, as we do all that has to be done.
Be with us, Lord, as we make time to meet you.

We are his people, he is our God.
Go with us now we pray.

God's joy be in our hearts
this Advent and for evermore. Amen.

May the God who sent his Son into the world go with us.
May the Son whom we remember at Christmas be with us.
May the Spirit who brings life to our lives stay with us. Amen.

Let us go to share the good news.
Let us go to spread the good news.
Let us go to live the good news. Amen.

We remember the birth of the Son.
Thank you, Jesus, for coming to us.
We look for the birth of the Son.
Thank you, Jesus, for coming to us.
We prepare for the birth of the Son.
Thank you, Jesus, for coming to us.